SHTF Prepping:

Survive & Thrive After A Disaster - Build A SHTF Stockpile, Create the Perfect Bug Out Bag, & Learn Off-Grid Survival Skills (SHTF Arsenal, SHTF Pantry, & Urban Prepping)

Kevin Gise © 2018

Disclaimer:

Introduction

The world is a tumultuous place. Our safety is far from guaranteed. Threats feel imminent on all sides. Whether man-made or due to mother nature, the danger is never far from our minds. If you want to be safe in a disaster, you must be prepared for anything. That's why it's referred to as an SHTF situation shortened from "Shit Hits The Fan." If you want to feel safe then you need to take the steps necessary to be ready. This book will show you how to prepare yourself and your family if an emergency occurs.

The worst case scenario can happen in the blink of an eye. One second you're fine and the next your world has been completely upended. These types of occurrences happen more often than you'd think. Every day people are displaced by violent uprisings, medical outbreaks, and natural disasters. Millions of people are forced to relocate each year and struggle to keep their family fed and safe. That it hasn't happened to you is no guarantee it won't down the road. That's why SHTF prepping is such an important part of any smart disaster preparedness plan.

We should hope for the world to remain safe and peaceful but we should always be ready if it isn't. I feel that's an intelligent way to live one's life. I'm hoping this guide will teach you a few of the lessons I've learned over the years and make getting prepared a smooth process. Everyone needs the same three items to survive. Those include water, food, and shelter. If you can't provide all three things, your chances of surviving an SHTF situation get dramatically lower. I'll discuss each of these things along with the importance of planning, creating the ideal bug out bags, preparing your SHTF pantry, defending yourself and your family, and learning the survival skills you might deem useful in the aftermath of an emergency.

Getting all of your projects and preps completed can take time, work, and money. The sooner you prep the more likely you'll be ready when the time comes. Don't drag your feet any longer. Get started today. It could make all the difference.

Let's begin!

Chapter One: An Intro to SHTF Prepping

SHTF Prepping Basics

Here is a prep list of things you'll want to do to get prepared for an SHTF situation. I'll go into more detail on a lot of these later throughout this book. This is just to give you an idea of the things you'll want to do.

1. Make a binder for your documents. You want to have this on hand. It's not only ideal for bigger SHTF situations, but it's also good for the small emergencies that happen to all of us. A few of the things to include are your social security cards, birth certificates, passports, marriage & divorce papers, mortgage & property insurance papers, health insurance papers & medical papers, diplomas, immunizations records, and a list of your prescriptions and important contact information. This binder needs to be somewhere that is safe but also easy to reach. My binder sits in a fireproof box that's in an accessible yet hidden safe.

2. Create your disaster and defense plan. You should know how you'll respond in an emergency. Whether it's defending your home from intrusion to bugging out to a new location. Be as detailed as possible. You should have multiple backup plans in place with directions laid out on what to do should a certain disaster occur. Have all your escape routes mapped out and alternate locations scouted.

3. Create a journal for your supplies and food. To begin, document everything that your family uses and eats during the week. You want this to be very thorough. Leave nothing out. Don't skip something you deem unimportant. An accurate representation of what you use and consume will allow you to make an accurate list for your food storage needs and long-term supplies.

4. Create a skills list. After you've come up with skills you think will come in handy, place them in order from the most to least important. Learn these skills in the order of their importance. A few skills to learn include gardening, self defense, first aid, weapons training, hunting, cooking, and navigation.

5. Inspect your home and vehicles. This is a thorough inspection. You should check every single inch of your home and vehicles. The aim is to find and repair any issues. You want to get these problem areas sorted out now before an emergency occurs and fixing things becomes exponentially harder.

6. Start your SHTF stockpile. Your stockpile should comprise of food, weapons, tools, household supplies, seeds, gardening supplies, gas, clothing, and other survival supplies. I would also consider stocking up on things to keep everyone entertained. This should include items like books, puzzles, and games. I would recommend that you stockpile medical books, cookbooks, DIY books, automotive books, gardening books, and home repair books. Once a disaster strikes you can't rely on someone else to help fix your problems. Having a collection of these books will allow you to try to solve the issue yourself.

7. Create bug out bags for yourself and anyone in your group. Each person needs their own bag and needs to know everything that's inside it. These bags have to be made beforehand, so if an SHTF situation occurs you can leave at the drop of a hat and still be ready.

8. If you live outside an urban environment with storage space, I suggest storing plenty of firewood. Having wood on hand as a source of fuel is important after a disaster. If a disaster strikes in the winter it could mean the difference between life and death. If you live in an urban environment with limited space, I suggest storing some additional propane and having portable heaters you can use in the case of an emergency.

9. Start exercising. Living off-grid requires a lot of physical work. The better shape you're in the easier it'll be to accomplish everything that needs to get done to survive. I enjoy hiking, boxing, and self-defense courses. It gives me a good mixture of physical activities and has allowed me to learn a new set of skills.

10. Create a first aid kit and dental kit. You want these to be as comprehensive as possible. When things turn ugly, you'll discover access to medicine and routine medical services will be hard to find. You should consider taking classes on basic medical assistance for things like minor injuries, burns, and open wounds. I would also get CPR certified.

SHTF Disaster Plan

Everyone serious about prepping for a disaster needs to have a plan in place. Without a solid plan and strategy, you'll miss important things that need to be in prepped and you might not recover. All it takes is a few things to go wrong and the chances of your survival will drop dramatically. Here is a list of questions you need to think about and answer before beginning.

How many will your group comprise of?

Where do you plan on taking shelter?

Have you considered a backup shelter in case your main shelter becomes compromised?

Will your shelter have access to a source of clean water that can be accessed easily?

Is your shelter fortified and secure from attackers?

Is your shelter dry and warm?

Is your food located at your shelter or do you need to go to another location to access it?

How long will your initial food supply last with the number of people in your group?

Is there a plan to keep your food safe and dry?

What is the plan for replenishing your stockpile once it's gone?

Will you be keeping multiple stockpiles in different locations?

Do you have a first aid kit and medicine stockpiled?

Does anyone in your group have medical training? If not, will one of you be getting some?

Do you have tools and supplies stockpiled for future use on projects?

Do you have weapons and a plan for defending yourself in place? Do you have escape routes planned?

Do you have any weapons training? If not, will one of you be getting some?

From this brief list of questions, you can see there are many factors to consider before creating your survival plan. Take time to answer the questions. Once you have, you can formulate a plan around your answers. You should always think of additional questions to be asking yourself. No list of questions is ever complete. However, the more questions you've asked yourself and answered the more prepared you'll be.

I separate my plan into three distinct stages. The first stage is called the short-term plan. This comprises of what steps I want to take during the initial four months of prepping. The second stage is called the mid-term plan, and this comprises of what steps I plan on taking after the short-term plan until about a year in. The third stage of my plan is the long-term plan and comprises of everything after a year of prepping. Each of these stages needs to be mapped out in advance so they can be properly prepared for. It's important to set deadlines and have detailed outlines of what needs to be done. Failing to do so could lead you to forget preps, waste preps you've already invested time in, or not finish preps because you've gotten lackadaisical with your time management.

Creating your stockpile is the easiest part. The difficult part involves understanding how long your rations will last, how they'll be used, and how you'll resupply them after an emergency occurs and they run low. I feel it's important to keep detailed records of each prep and each item that's part of the stockpile. You need to know the quantity of every item, when they were added, when they will expire, any instructions on using them, and a schedule for food rotation so that nothing ever gets unnecessarily wasted.

The more thorough your records and the more care you take in overseeing your stockpile, the greater your chance at surviving off-grid indefinitely. This process can overwhelm, but I promise they are easy habits to pick up once you get going. Don't wait too long before starting your stockpile. You'll need all the time you can get.

Don't keep the only record of your preps online. You need to have a physical copy of your records when an emergency happens. Remember, you're likely to lose access to your Internet and power during an SHTF situation. If you can't access your prepping records, then all your work and planning will have been done for nothing. I have four copies of my records. One is kept off-site with additional preps, one is kept in my safe, one is kept in my bug out bag, and one is kept in the trunk of my vehicle.

You need to make more than a single plan. There's a good chance your plan could get compromised depending on the emergency. You need to have different plans for different situations. You must have your main escape routes and alternates in case those become blocked off. I suggest scouting out multiple bug out locations in different directions from your home and hide a few supplies stockpiles along each of the escape routes. Contingencies are a vital part of any disaster plan. The more options you have the higher your chance of survival. I have created multiple plans and strategies for each type of disaster situation. This allows me to have plans that are tailored to the situation. I keep a bug out bag stored in each direction a few miles from my home. This way if I'm driven out of my home in a certain direction I know I'll have supplies that are accessible.

Always be drilling your different plans. It's important that you can put your plan into motion without hesitation. The best plan in the world won't mean much if you're not able to execute it. I was shocked at how I performed when first drilling. I realized my plans had flaws that needed to be corrected. It took repetition but now my family and I are ready to put our plan in motion at a moments notice. I like to hold drills at random times to keep everyone on point. Remember, dealing with an emergency is more difficult when you are feeling the effects of fear and stress. Drill until you know your disaster plans front to back. You should hold drills a minimum of once a month. I suggest holding them more often when first starting. Don't be afraid to change or improve any parts of your plans that don't meet your expectations.

Chapter Two: Food & Water = Survival

Water Storage Basics

Water is essential for our survival. Your body requires a certain amount of water to function. Water is not only used for drinking, it's also important for growing food, cleaning, cooking, and washing. Every SHTF stockpile needs to place a big emphasis on water storage. You need to create a detailed plan on how you will replenish your water once your supply runs dry. You need to choose a location that has a reliable source of clean water. This spot also needs to be secure and easily defended. Learn about locating water sources and how to filter the water you find.

Plan for each person in your group to use about 1 gallon of water a day. This will allow you to get a rough estimate of how long the water can last. Once you've gone through the process of getting water and running dry a few times, you can get a better estimation of how long the water will last.

Find multiple nearby water sources if possible. This way if one gets contaminated you'll still have other sources of water to fall back on. Make sure each of your bug out locations are close to a clean water source. The more options you have, the more you'll be able to pivot. I would suggest always carrying water on you whenever going out after an emergency. This way if you get delayed or stuck you'll have additional time to get home or extricate yourself from the problem without having to be concerned about finding water.

Invest in a rainwater collector and high-end filter for your home. This will give you the ability to use the filtered rainwater to do chores like cleaning your clothes or washing. You don't want to use your drinking water if you don't need to. I would also consider purchasing smaller portable filters for your bug out bag or that you can bring with you when venturing out.

You should have between 150 and 200 gallons of long-term water storage. If you don't have the room store as much as your space will allow. I have close to 400 gallons of water storage. I keep it in large 50-gallon stainless steel containers I stack up vertically in rows next to one another. I have them stacked two high and four wide. I had plenty of space on my property so having the extra storage wasn't an issue. Use the setup that works best for your situation. The key takeaway is that you have a storage system in place.

Common Water Storage Myths

Here are myths about water storage and the corresponding facts.

1. Water has to be treated before being stored. There's a belief that your tap water will need treatment before it's stored. This is false. Tap water located almost anywhere in the United States is safe and you need not do anything when initially storing it in containers. It's already been filtered and purified when it went through the treatment plant. It's fine for storage. Remember, there's little point in treating water beforehand as water will grow microorganisms when stored for a long time. You should always treat your water before you're getting close to using it. Treating it before storage and after storage is not a good use of your time. I always treat my water with a higher efficiency filter. These can remove nearly 100% of the organisms growing in your water along with any pollution and dirt.

2. Having barrels or a water tank will keep me prepared no matter what. This is false. Having barrels and tanks are excellent solutions for storing large amounts of water. However, if you need to bug out from your location, you won't be able to take these massive tanks and barrels with you. It's smart to keep other size water containers filled and ready to go. I keep a few 5-gallon containers ready for use if I'm forced to bug out in my vehicle. If I have to leave on foot, I keep a few canteens and a small portable hydration system ready. It's not enough to have a one size fits all solution. With something as important as water you need to have multiple options ready at your disposal.

3. Water storage isn't necessary since I have access to a well or clean water source nearby. This is false. Just because you have access to water now doesn't mean those sources will be available later. Depending on the SHTF situation, your water source might become undrinkable. At that point, you'd have cornered yourself and your family into a dangerous predicament. You need to have control over your water supply and safe access. Storing water is the only way to make sure you have both things.

4. You can store water in any container. This is mostly false. In an emergency, you can use any clean container for short-term storage. However, for storing water long-term you have to be a little smarter about the containers you choose. Many containers aren't built for long-term use. They will degrade over the course of a few months and chemicals from the container will dissolve into the water. These containers will eventually leak and become useless. An example of this is milk jugs. You also don't want a clear container as they let light in which helps foster organisms to grow. Ideally, you'd want a plastic barrel that is food-grade quality. These barrels are normally blue and block most light from getting in. The higher quality water container you choose the safer your water supply will be.

5. Water will go bad over time. This is false. Water is comprised of H2O and that's it. It can be stored for years and will still hydrate you the way it would if it was stored for days. I always keep a fresh supply of about 10 gallons on hand so I can have a sufficient amount to drink straight out of the container. It'd be a pain in the butt to filter and treat your water every time you wanted a glass.

Filtering & Treating Water

When locating a water source you need to purify and filter the water that comes from it. Drinking toxic or contaminated water can lead to illness and death. Be careful not to drink any water that could be unsanitary.

1. Be Wary Of Chemicals - Filtering and purifying water that has been contaminated by chemicals will not work. If you think there could be chemicals in the water you need to locate an alternate water source.

2. Boiling Water - Boiling water is the normal way to purify water. Between boiling and filtering water, you've destroyed nearly all organisms growing in it. Boil your water for 3 minutes if you have a lot on hand and 1 minute if you're running low and are at sea level. Boiling water causes water to evaporate so don't boil it longer than I've recommended.

3. Coffee Filter - I always keep coffee filters in my bug out bags and SHTF pantry. These are perfect for filtering water before boiling it. The filter will gather up most of the sediment and debris. You always need to filter your water. Sand, charcoal, and gravel can also help filter water.

4. Chemical Treatment - You can buy chemical purification tablets that will help get rid of viruses, bacteria, and other hygienic issues. These tablets are great because they are easy to use and have a longer shelf life. I always keep these in my bug out bags and SHTF pantry.

Ways to Store Water

Water isn't safe to drink because it's clear. Parasites, organisms, and chemicals are usually colorless. Be sure to always treat your water before drinking.

If possible, you should try to rotate your water at least once a year. This will keep it fresher and free of a lot of chemicals and microorganisms. Don't just toss your rotated water out. It's still great for bathing, dishes, laundry, and watering plants.

I've mentioned this early but don't store your water in anything except food grade containers. Don't use cheap buckets or biodegradable bottles. To determine if a container is food grade ready it will be made of #1, 2, 4, 7 plastic. This number will be found in the triangle recycle symbol on the bottom of the container. It will also tell you if the container is safe to be frozen or stored in your pantry. Never use a food grade container that was used for something else. Please buy your water containers new. Even trace amounts of certain things will taint the water within. If you're going to use a metallic container, make sure its stainless steel. Anything else will corrode. This will lead to disgusting rusty water.

Never use a container that can't be sealed. Water shouldn't be stored out in the open. Particles and other nasty things will get into your water supply. If you think a container has been compromised, you need to replace it. Make sure you don't store your container directly in the sun or next to a heat source. Your storage area needs to be a shaded area. Temperature controlled garages, basements, and cellars are all good spots for storing water long-term.

1. Plastic Containers - This is the best storage option for most people. It is easy to find, cheaper than other options, durable, and lightweight. On the negative side, some scientists believe plastic will leach chemicals into your water over time. This process is sped up if left in the heat or direct sunlight. This problem can be avoided by replacing the water occasionally.

2. Stainless Steel Containers - The only type of steel one should use to store water in. Considered the safest option for long-term water storage. No chance of chemicals leaching into your water. Stainless steel containers are also incredibly durable and help protect water from sunlight. Your container must be food grade. You also want to avoid storing water that was treated using chlorine as that will erode all the protective surfaces on your container and lead to corrosion. On the negative side, these containers are the most expensive and the heaviest of your options.

3. Glass Containers - A trusted storage option. You need to sanitize the container before putting in your water. You need to use new containers only. Glass is marked by the FDA under the designation "G.R.A.S" or "Generally Regarded As Safe." These containers can last forever, can be washed and sterilized, and are easy to find. On the negative side, they are heavy to move around and are prone to breaking. You can help reduce the odds of breaking a container by wrapping it in newspaper and a little cardboard.

4. Water Blatters - These are good for storing water in an emergency. This blatter is a refillable bag that can be placed in your sink, tub, or shower and be filled with water without being afraid it will get contaminated. It can hold up to 100 gallons and is easy to empty and pack for transportation. These are cheap and it's a smart idea to keep a few of these in your SHTF stockpile. On the negative side, these are not a permanent long-term solution and are only meant for short-term use.

5. 55-Gallon Plastic Water Barrels - These are good as a long-term storage solution. These barrels are reliable and are much cheaper than the stainless steel option. They are blue to block out the light. On the negative side, they are extremely difficult to move once full and will take up a lot of room. These are a step-down safety wise from the steel containers but if you're on a budget, these will work with minimal exposure to risk.

6. The Pool - This is for emergency situations only. If you've run low on water, you can drink water from a pool if it's been properly treated. If you want to consider your pool as a source of water you need to have a good filtration and purification plan in advance. This can get you through a short period but you need to find a more reliable source of water long-term. On the negative side, if treated with too many chemicals this water can be poisonous. Pools are open and therefore home to more insects and other bacteria. The water needs to be chemically treated or boiled before drinking as a safety precaution.

7. Water Wells - Wells help to store and produce water. If you're able to have one on your property, it can be a nice source of drinkable water. On the negative side, your well could become contaminated like any rivers or ponds nearby in certain SHTF situations. You would still need another water storage system along with a well.

8. Water Cisterns - An excellent long-term water solution. These are large and expensive pieces that can't be moved around once they're in place. If you have one of these on your property, you should be good on usable drinking water for a long time. A cistern is able to hold from between 250 and 10,000+ gallons of water depending on its size. On the negative side, they require a big undertaking to set up and get put into place. Once it's been installed you can't move it or take it with you if you ever need to bug out.

9. Plastic Water Bottles - These are only a short-term water solution. It's a cheap way to get water, but the plastic is biodegradable and will break down over time leaching chemicals into the water. You should always have portable water storage options on hand but if you go with bottles, they must be rotated often.

Growing & Raising Your Own Food

Most people take their food supply for granted. In an emergency, our supply of food would disappear quicker than you'd think. That's why it's important to be prepared for a situation where access to outside food is cut off. Even in a short-term situation, it could lead to starvation.

The more land you have the more food you'll be able to cultivate and grow. I enjoy growing my food and sourcing nearby farms for food. I feel it tastes better than anything I can buy from a store. Even if you don't have a lot of room on your property, you still can grow a decent amount of food from just a tiny vegetable and herb garden. The idea is to learn how to fend for yourself and provide your own food while also storing it long-term in the event of a disaster.

Another good benefit of growing your own food is that it can lead to significant cost savings and allow you to have additional money for other supplies you need. After your garden is producing, you can cut your food bill way down. You should have a plan mapped out before beginning your garden. This way you know what you plan on growing for everyday use and what types of food you plan to grow and store long-term in your SHTF pantry. Growing your food is hard work but worth it. It will give your family the food security it deserves and will set you up for success in case of an SHTF situation.

Before you begin on your garden, you must decide your technique for gardening. There are a lot of options to choose from. You should read books on gardening, taking into account the climate you live in. Some foods thrive better in certain areas of the world. It's good to know the information in advance so you can plan accordingly. I use bio-intensive gardening. It allows me to produce a much higher yield than I might get by using a different technique.

Eight Principles of Bio-Intensive Gardening:

1. Composting

2. Intensive Planting

3. Deep Soil Preparation

4. Companion Planting

5. Growing Crops for Grains & Carbons

6. Using Open Pollinated Seeds

7. Growing High-Calorie Crops in Small-Sized Areas

8. Integrating These Processes Into One Interrelated System

Since I use this form of gardening, I double dig all my garden beds and all the compost I use was made from a crop that was used for that purpose. A few of those crops, corn as one example, will also yield food. Using the principles in unison builds a system that is balanced. It feeds the soil and improves the whole ecosystem in the process.

You should stick to the method you find appealing. Be sure to maintain extensive records and map out the amount of food you must grow in advance. Keeping excellent records will allow you to see how your gardening is going over time and will give you the information to refine the process and make improvements. You'll know the exact amount of food grown, what foods you grew too little or too much of, and a bunch of other helpful information.

Remember, you need to grow a few staple crops. These foods are crucial to your diet. You also need to grow food you can easily harvest and store each season. You want to focus on foods that will give you a big yield and are high in calories.

Types Of Food to Grow

Wheat - This will let you make enough bread to feed your family all year. It will also give you something valuable to trade or barter.

Herb & Vegetable Garden - I grow tomatoes, cabbage, peppers, kale, celery, cucumbers, and carrots in my garden. I also grow a lot of my favorite herbs. Grow whatever fruits, veggies, and herbs you prefer.

Potatoes & Sweet Potatoes - A good source of extra calories that can be made into a variety of dishes. Potatoes are simple to grow and safely keep stored. Potatoes normally grow in 65 to 85 days depending on the potato being grown.

Dry Beans - Beans come in a variety of options. Particular beans will grow better in specific types of climates. Beans are the perfect staple food. They provide a lot of calories and taste delicious. Dry beans are simple to keep stored long-term. A perfect food for SHTF preppers.

Grain Corn - Grain corn comes in a variety of options. Particular strains will grow better in specific types of climates. Grain corn can be turned into cornmeal, which can make items like bread, polenta, pancakes, and pudding.

Animals to Own for Food

Having your own animals will come in handy if you're ever forced to live off-grid for an extended period. They can provide milk, eggs, meat, and wool. If you get an animal and decide you don't want it, you always have the option of selling it to a person who does.

Here's a list of animals you should consider.

Sheep (Milk, Meat, & Wool) - These are friendly creatures that can provide a source of milk, wool, and meat.

Chickens (Eggs & Meat) - Chickens can produce a constant source of eggs and are great for their meat. Chickens require little maintenance. The main issue is plucking your chicken once it's ready to be eaten. Purchase a mechanical plucker to save you the hassle.

Rabbits (Meat) - Rabbits are a nice source of meat and are simpler to process than a chicken.

Ducks (Eggs & Meat) - Ducks lay large-sized eggs and are good for their meat. Ducks require little maintenance.

Beef Cattle (Meat) - A single large-sized beef cattle will fill up your freezer for an entire season.

Milk Cow (Milk) - Milk cows offer a constant stream of milk and cream. Great items to trade and barter with.

Goats (Milk, Cheese, & Meat) - Animals that can be hard to keep a track of if not securely fenced in. Goats are known for the milk and cheese they can provide. They also provide a nice source of meat. Goats also help to clear any land that has become overgrown where they live.

Owning and taking care of animals is an important job. I suggest beginning with an animal or two and growing from there. Always research the animals you purchase before buying. You're responsible for their safety and well-being. You don't want to harm your investment because you couldn't be bothered to care for them the right way. Treat your animals well and they will reward you for years to come.

Long-Term Food Storage

Long-term storage is necessary to survive an SHTF situation that lasts for a long period. Food and water storage is the key to ensuring your survival. That's why planning out what you need to prep in advance is so vital. If you miss something you must do without it. There's no driving to the supermarket in an SHTF situation.

I turned a room in my house into a fully stocked water and food storage area. I have a shelving unit system in place for my food and large steel containers holding my water supply. Having set this all up before any issues provides me with comfort as I know that I've taken steps to be prepared for an emergency. With all my preps tracked I can easily track my water and food, making changes as needed. Always choose a space that is cool and dry. Don't pick a place that is too hot or too cold. You don't want an area that is wet or damp. This will lead to mold growing on your food and could be disastrous to your food supply.

To choose foods to store for long periods, you have to know the foods that will last long-term. You should also consider learning how to can your food, preserve your food, and cure your meat. Don't forget to rotate your food before it expires.

Here are basic food items perfect for long-term storage.

These items can last almost indefinitely.

Raw Honey

White Sugar

Brown Sugar

Salt

Alcohol

Hard Grains can last for 10 to 12 years.

Hard Red Wheat

Millet

Dry Corn

Soft White Wheat

Durum wheat

Buckwheat

Spelt

Kamut

Beans that are sealed can last for 8 to 10 years.

Adzuki Beans

Lentils

Garbanzo Beans

Pinto Beans

Black Turtle Beans

Lima Beans

Kidney Beans

Soft Grains that are sealed can last for 7 to 8 years.

Oats

Barley

Quinoa

Rye

Mixes, Flours, & Pasta that can last for 5 to 8 years.

White Rice

White Flour

Pasta

Whole Wheat Flour

Coconut Oil

Cornmeal

All-Purpose Flour

Fruits & Veggies that can be stored for 2 months or more.

Apples

Sweet Potato

Dry Beans

Pear

Rutabaga

Onion

Carrots

Garlic

Shallot

Celery

Turnip

Winter Squash

Beet

Grain corn

Parsnip

Pumpkin

Cabbage

Leek

Potato

Miscellaneous items that can last for 2 to 5 years

Peanut Butter

Canned Meats

Dried Herbs & Spices

Fruits

Canned Tuna

Tea

Canned Vegetables

Coffee

Hard Candy

Powdered milk

There are many foods available for long-term storage. Try to keep your food pantry stocked and prepped for an emergency. These food items will give you a lot of flexibility in the meals you'll be able to prepare. Even if you have animals and your garden is producing food it's good to have food items in reserve. You never know when a bad winter will kill crops or disease will kill off animals.

Have your system for storing food ready before beginning your preps. This will help you save both energy and time. When a system isn't in place, it'll be hard to track the food you have, what food you need more of, and when food is set to expire. Everything gets labeled with the name of the food item, the date it was placed into storage, and when it's about to expire. I have a ledger that keeps all my information handy and accessible. Don't forget to rotate your food, placing items with longer expiration dates at the back and moving up any food about to expire.

Chapter Three: Prepping In An Urban Environment

Urban Prepping Guide

SHTF prepping takes many forms. Someone in an urban environment will prep differently from someone in a rural or suburban area. In an urban area, the amount of people per square mile is much higher. You'll have less room to work with and your planning needs to be precise. In an urban environment, the odds are after an SHTF disaster you'll be forced to bug out. You won't have the room to store enough preps to live long-term and finding freshwater sources will be difficult. I suggest you figure out a more remote location to bug out to if you live in an urban setting. This way you'll have more room and privacy. It will give you a much better chance at survival. Scout for locations near multiple water sources and areas prime for hunting and gardening.

Here are a few tips for prepping and dealing with an SHTF situation in an urban environment.

1. Once the power goes out gather up as much water as you can. I would suggest investing in a few water blatters and fill up your sinks and tub. If you're bugging in fill up every glass, bottle, bucket, and bowl with water. If you're bugging out make sure you've got as much water as you can comfortably take with you.

2. Know every route to get out of where you live. In an SHTF situation, people lose it and things will turn bad. Keep a bug out bag handy and make sure your bug out location has been chosen and scouted. A smart way to leave is by following abandoned railroads out of your city or town.

3. Be smart when searching for food. In cities, a few places to check include vending machines, office buildings that have cafeterias, closed gyms and restaurants. These places will have less competition than convenience stores and supermarkets.

4. Avoid fighting with other people. People get into an agitated state when an emergency occurs. Don't get pulled into unnecessary conflicts. If you get injured or killed what will happen to the people depending on you.

5. Invest in solar. When you live in a small apartment, you can find a ton of ways to limit the power you need to take from the grid. If you're looking into bugging in, it is important that you can survive without access to electricity.

6. Don't show other people your walkie-talkies or weapons when outside the home. People will target you for your weapons and preps. Letting people know you're a prepper will turn you into a target.

7. Keep a carry kit with you at all times. This is a small kit that can make a big difference in an urban disaster. This kit should be compromised of a bottle of water, a Bic lighter, cash, a folding knife, a portable radio, and a good multi-tool.

8. Don't rely on your car when creating a bug out plan. Most likely the city will become gridlocked before you leave. This might leave you trapped in the center of riots and people looting. Avoid people as much as you can during an urban SHTF situation.

9. Keep a little gear on hand aimed at protection during an environmental SHTF situation. This will include lung protection, hand protection, eye protection, and hearing protection.

10. Don't bring unnecessary attention to you and your family. Don't wear camouflage out in public during a disaster. You don't want people to think you've prepared for an emergency. If people think you have supplies, they'll try to take them from you.

11. When bugging in don't go by your windows. You don't want people knowing your home. It will make you a target for desperate people. It's a small safety measure but an important one.

There are many things to prepare for when urban prepping. If you're bugging in while living in an urban setting you need to research and make your home and preps as efficient as possible for a long-term stay. It's not something I recommend doing but if you don't have many other options, it's best to be ready.

Essential Urban Survival Gear

Dust Mask - You might need protection from airborne particles or debris.

Multi-Tool - A good multi-tool like a Leatherman Wingman allows you the ability to accomplish small jobs and solve minor issues.

Pry Bar / Crow Bar - Good for removing debris, barriers, hammering glass, and scavenging. These come in all sizes and varieties.

Vitamins - You'll be restricted in your food choices. Having a good multi-vitamin will allow you to get all the nutrients and vitamins you need to stay healthy.

Medication - You need to make sure you have your prescription medication along with a general first aid kit.

Work Gloves - You'll need a sturdy pair to work in. These will keep your hands safe.

Urban Axe - Versatile and powerful tool in your arsenal. It can be used as a hatchet, knife, and pick axe. These can also close and open gas mains and water hydrants. It also serves as an effective weapon.

Can Opener - You'll need to open plenty of canned food if you plan on surviving in an urban setting long-term. This will make life much easier.

Metal Spork - The perfect food tool. You want to have one on hand.

Permanent Marker - Good if you want to leave a note or marking for yourself or other people to see.

Essential Urban Survival Kit Weapons

Firearm - You want to consider owning a gun and learn how to safely operate it. You never know what situation you'll find yourself in after an emergency.

Knife - A knife is a great weapon for self-defense. Can also be used for a variety of other things.

Pepper Spray - A good choice for deterring an attacker without causing permanent damage.

Surviving An Urban Disaster Situation

If you decide not to bug in during an urban disaster and want to travel and scavenge without a plan, you'll need to consider a few things. I don't suggest trying this but if you do; you want to think of where to go, when to move, and what to wear.

Find the nearest wooded region. So why the woods? Isn't that away from the food and shelter? While that's true it's also away from people. That's the big danger in any city. People grouped together gravitate towards a gang mentality and then anything is likely to happen. Most of it isn't good.

Try to stay on the outskirts of the city when you're not in the woods. You want to blend in with people. Don't wear camouflage or other things that will make you stand out. Try wearing urban camouflage. That means you wear clothes that look like normal street wear but are practical in the woods. You should dress to match the season. No winter coats in summer. A good example of urban camo is a brown T-shirt, trail shoes, green pants and a black pullover. Once you get out of the populated areas, you can take off the black pullover and you're in camouflage.

Try keeping your movement on foot to only specific times of the day. Those are dusk and early evening. You still have light to guide the way and you don't have to risk using your flashlight. If you get stuck in the city and need a place to sleep find a good rooftop or multiple story building for cover. Most predators don't think to gaze up when they are hunting. If the weather is bad, you should locate an abandoned building and find a secure location inside with a few different avenues of escape.

Chapter Four: Building A Bug Out Bag & Surviving When Off-Grid Living

Creating The Perfect Bug Out Bag

Create the optimal bug out bag is important. Every person in your group has to have their own bug out bag. I keep each bag stocked exactly the same, except for individual clothing items.

The first step is deciding on your bug out bag. I use the Osprey Atmos 65 backpack but there are plenty of other ones to choose from. This backpack gives me the space I need to fit all my items without weighing me down. The bag weighs 30lbs with all the items packed, including a tent. The weight won't account for any additional water or food I bring. I went through 4 different bags until I got one I was comfortable with.

I made a few changes to my backpack. I removed the original internal bags and replaced them with ultralight bags. I did this to lower the weight. To cut down on the amount of space used in my backpack, I use packing cubes to keep everything organized. I have a few types of bags for my gear. I keep a medical bag, toiletries bag, survival tools bag, tent bag, electronics bag, cooking set bag, and sleeping bag. I label each of these bags so they are easy to find. Before you pack, lay all your items out and check to be sure nothing is missing. You don't want to forget this step. You never want to be put in a situation where you've forgotten an important item. It could have disastrous results.

Here is a breakdown of the bags and their contents. Your situation may require you to add or subtract certain items. This is a guideline but tailor your bags to what works for you and your family. Your budget, location, and skills will all play a part in what will make it into your bug out bag.

Electronics Bag

Phone & Charger

Encrypted Thumb Drive (Documents Binder & Personal Info)

Laptop or Tablet & Charger

Ham Radio & Charger

Batteries (Every Size)

Sleeping Bag / Tent

Choose the brand you want. They should be lightweight, durable, waterproof and fit the size requirements you require. I pack a sleeping bag, tarp, tent, wool blanket, and ground pad in each bug out bag.

Medical Bag

Prescription Medications

Bandages (Variety of Sizes)

Neosporin

Tylenol / Advil

Combat Gauze

Moleskin

Sunscreen

Tourniquet

Compress

Survival Tools Bag

Handgun + Ammo (Only for people trained to use them)

Folding Pocket Knife

Emergency Mylar Blanket

Lighters

Matches & Fire Starter

Multi-Tool

Duct Tape

Maps (Mark Your Bug Out Locations & Rendezvous Locations)

Mini Filtration System & Straw

Snare Wire

Paracord

Candles

Scissors

Fishing Kit

Adjustable Wrench

Tape Measure

Pepper Spray

Rope Tightener

Sewing Kit

Headlamp w/ Extra Battery

Signal Mirror

Flashlight & Night Vision Filter

Key Chain Light

Binoculars

Chainsaw w/ Additional Hand

Hatchet

S Clips

Crank Power Charger

Clothing Bag

Dry Base Layer Pants

Polyester Long Sleeve Shirt

Boots (1 Pair)

Socks (Multiple Pairs)

Shoes (1 Pair)

Pants (Multiple)

Jacket or Fleece

Underwear (Multiple)

Shirts (Multiple)

Wool Hat

Waterproof Rain Gear

Work Gloves

Cooking Set

Trangia Alcohol Stove w/ Yellow Heet

Wood Burning Backpacking Stove

Spork

Titanium Pot w/ Frying Pan Lid

Metal Cup

Metal Plate

Pot Holder

Folding Spatula

Sugar

Can Opener

MRE's

Pot Scrubber

Water Purification Tablets

Salt

Pepper

Toiletries Bag

Liquid Soap

Shampoo

Aloe Vera

Toilet Paper

Toothbrushes

Toothpaste

Wet Napkins

Hand Sanitizer

Chapstick

Antacid

Gold Bond Body Powder

Ear Plugs

Dental Floss

Water & Food

The last addition to your bug out bag is your water and food
rations. Your body needs a minimum of 1 liter of water each
day. I try to bring a few more liters than I think I'll need. This
is one instance where the additional weight is all right. For
your food rations, you want enough for 3 to 4 days. I always
pack MRE's, protein bars, chewing gum, and hard cady in my
bag. I usually keep 5 MRE's and 10 protein bars in the bag.
This is enough to get me through 5 to 6 days.

Bugging Out

If you need to bug out, you'll want to have a destination to
travel to figured out in advance. This location needs to be
stocked with supplies. If an SHTF situation occurs, you need a
few alternate evacuation routes to safety. Not preparing
yourself beforehand will put you and your family in a
precarious position. If you can't find a safe place to ride out
the emergency, you'll run into trouble quickly.

My favorite acronym describing the steps when bugging out is
the term "LAST OUT."

L stands for location.

A stands for alternative routes.

S stands for supplies.

T stands for timing.

O stands for Observation.

U stands for uniformity.

T stands for transportation.

Let's go through each of these a little more.

Location

In an ideal scenario, you'll bug out with your family and loved ones. However, you could be apart at the time of the SHTF situation and be forced to find one another. That's why it's important that everyone knows your rendezvous location in the case of an emergency. Everyone should also know the final destination in case they get delayed or stopped from reaching the initial rendezvous location. Some people keep small HAM radios in their car for communication in these situations.

Alternative Routes

You need multiple routes mapped out and multiple rendezvous points along the route to your final bug out location. The first route is your best option if mass panic hasn't occurred and the roads are still open. You should avoid big cities and large towns. It's all right to travel through small-sized towns.

The next route will not only go over how to get to your final location avoiding every major city and town but also smaller towns. This includes bridges, tunnels, gorges, mountains or bodies of water. This can be a difficult route to map out but it's crucial that you do so even if it requires a ton of work planning.

Rendezvous locations are critical. Every route needs a few of these in the event your group gets separated or you have to pivot to a different place because the area became compromised. You need the ability to adjust the route from each rendezvous location so you'll still be able to get to your final destination.

I have all my maps and schedules in sealed tubes I place in all the vehicles my family owns. I also keep an additional copy in every bug out bag. This information is important and I treat it that way. Be sure to practice your route in advance on multiple occasions. I find the repetition makes learning the route much easier than by looking at a map with no good frame of reference. Make sure everyone in your group takes part in the drills involving your route. Each person needs to know the rendezvous points, bug out location, and how to go about getting there safely.

Supplies

I like my bugs to weigh between 30lbs and 35lbs. This weight allows me to fit everything I need along with some additional food and water. These bug out bags are still light enough to travel with and won't slow us down too much.

Timing

The right timing is key to your survival. It is an aspect that is often forgotten about. Once you realize you're in an SHTF situation and your location has been compromised, you need to bug out. If you wait you risk getting trapped, injured, separated from your group, or even killed. It's better you leave too soon and be wrong, then waiting too long. Being wrong just means you got an extra opportunity to practice your run. A little more experience will only help you in the long run.

Observation & Intel

Always be observing the area around you. You need to be an expert at gathering information and seeing patterns. These skills will pay off in an SHTF situation. You'll be able to make smarter and quicker decisions regarding your travel. Keeping these skills sharp will also give you a better idea of when an SHTF situation may be about to happen. Remember, the more of a head start you can get the better off you'll be.

Uniformity

Your group having the same preps is important to your survival. Everyone needs access to the same things. If people in your group all have different preps, certain things may get overlooked, ending in disorganization and severe consequences.

Transportation

How will you get around after a disaster strikes, During most emergencies a truck or car won't get you very far due to road congestion, raised bridges, destroyed roadways, blockades, and a variety of other hazards.

Motorcycles can make more sense but aren't viable if traveling with your loved ones. There's also no ability to hold extra gear or gas. You could modify the bike, adding a few saddlebags, but you still wouldn't have a lot of additional space for your gear.

Boats will work in certain scenarios. You need to have access to water and a location that can be accessed by water. You'll also need extra parts and fuel. You'll also want to take a few classes in boat repair in case you ever find yourself broken down.

Planes and helicopters are smart options but not a practical reality for most of us.

The majority of people will end up going in their vehicle as far as they're able to. And then travel by foot the rest of the time. This is the lengthiest and most arduous way to proceed but gives you flexibility and the chance to go unseen when running into other groups of people.

Surviving After You've Bugged Out

You prepped correctly and made it to your bug out location, now you need to survive. It's harder than it seems. Staying calm and in control under pressure can be difficult.

The way you initially react will have an impact on your ability to survive long-term.

Here are a list things you'll need to consider if you want to survive long-term.

1. Securing Your Area - Check the perimeter of your camp and determine the key features of the surrounding terrain. Locate a good vantage point to view the area around you. Make notes of water, trails, train tracks, and roads. Take all these assessments and determine if the area is safe to stay in. Keep an eye out for tracks of other people traveling through. Listen for voices and footsteps. If you've scouted an area because it has a lot of resources other people might have done the same thing.

2. Assessing the Emotional & Physical Health of Everyone In Your Group - Giving everyone in your party a full evaluation is important. Small injuries can become life-threatening if not treated and if a person is traumatized by the disaster you need to be aware before you put your life and safety in their hands. If there are injuries in your group treat the most severe cases first and work backward from there. I suggest learning CPR and first aid training to be properly prepared. Take great care with children to understand their state of mind once things have calmed down, and the adrenaline has worn off. You should prepare everyone mentally beforehand so that they're able to better handle an emergency once it occurs.

3. Attempt to Set Up Communication - You want to learn what is happening after you've bugged out. Try listening for emergency broadcasts on your radio. They can provide much need information on the damage done and expected outlook. This type of information will allow you to make a decision on whether to stay in your current location or start planning for a move somewhere else. Don't rely on your cell phones for communication. More than likely the lines will be down after a disaster. If your phone does work, conserve your battery using it only a few minutes at a time.

4. Prepare & Set Up Your Camp - Build a shelter, start a fire, and work on preserving your food. I always keep multiple means of starting a fire. You never know what the weather will be. You need to set aside an area as the bathroom and another one for washing. Hygiene is important. You don't want to want to risk getting sick. Your bathroom should be about 200 feet away from the camp and somewhere downhill from your location. I suggest building a latrine. Dig out a 6 foot trench that is 8-inches deep. Cover the waste with soil as it's used. When you've used all the space, choose another area. Too much waste in an area will attract wildlife and decrease the rate it decomposes at. When it comes to your food, be sure to keep it away from animals. I suggest hanging it in the air about 15 feet high. Take a thick stick and tie a rope to the end of it. Toss it over a high branch and tie your food bag at the other end. Hoist the bag up into the air and secure the end to the tree trunk.

5. Find Water - You should have planned to bug out to a spot near water. Use this water supply but purify any water before drinking it. If you aren't near a water source, you must get creative. You can harvest water by tapping into plants and trees., collecting your condensed water using a transpiration bag. You can also dig out for water in low points of the terrain by looking for indicators like a line of shrub plants.

6. Ration Out Your Supplies - Figure out your food supply in advance and determine the maximum time you can stretch out your food reserves to survive. You can check charts for minimum daily calorie requirements to determine this correctly. You should pack plenty of dehydrated foods, protein bars, and MRE's.

7. Search for Food - This includes hunting game, foraging for plants, & preparing a garden. You'll want to learn how to set traps for small game and how to track larger game. You'll also want to learn how to forage for food. There are plenty of plants that are edible. Be careful, there are also a lot that are poisonous. Learn the difference between edible and poisonous plants in advance to avoid this problem. You can also try fishing for food. Whatever your method it's important you begin searching for food as soon as you can. Your supplies might not last you for long depending on the amount of prepping you've done.

8. Set Up Your Camp Defenses - Set up a system of trip wires around your camp. You also want to set up a watch. Someone should always be on lookout. You can also gather any thorny bush in the area and turn it into a makeshift fence around your camp. You should also have plans in place on how to deal with human intruders. Have easy access to your weapons and assign everyone a different responsibility in the event of an attack. Stay level-headed and calm. Making smart decisions could mean the difference between life and death.

Chapter Five: Surviving When Bugging In

Surviving When Bugging In

Big disasters like tornadoes, hurricanes, floods, and even large winter storms can bring life to a halt. These emergencies can pose a large danger and create widespread devastation and damage. Important services like electricity and water can become interrupted, leaving people without light, heat, or waste services. Traveling any distance can become close to impossible. Normal luxuries like gas stations, hospitals, and convenience stores become inaccessible.

Dealing with this set of conditions will require planning and preparation. Bugging in will be the best option for most families in these emergencies. Even the government suggests you should have a minimum of 3 days supply in the event of a survival emergency. I like to consider that as a starting point. I continue to add supplies expanding the size of my SHTF pantry. Prepping for an emergency can take a lot of work but your safety and the safety of your loved one is worth it.

Be sure to drill your emergency plans. Everyone needs to play their part in the event of a disaster. The more people understand their role and responsibilities the calmer they'll be able to respond when under pressure. Your plan should include gathering any pets and family members inside, charging all of your electronic devices and keeping them fully charged as long as you can, setting up communication to get the latest news as it unfolds. Every family should have an emergency kit easy to access. This kit should have a crank or battery operated radio, a flashlight, extra batteries, matches, candles, a lighter, a knife, a multi-tool, cash, and a supply of any medicines that are taken by the people in your family. Keep these items stored in a box or bag and store it with a first aid kit in an area that everyone knows is designated for your emergency supplies.

The moment you know an emergency is probable or already unfolding your disaster plan goes into effect. If you don't receive or hear about an evacuation order be ready to hunker down and bug in. Check all communication channels to make sure it's all right to remain in your area. If you've done all your prep work in advance, you should be in a good position to ride out the emergency.

1. Select Your Designated Shelter

The first concern when bugging in is to determine your shelter hub. You need to stay dry, warm, and safe from the elements. You need to pick a room or area of your home you designate as your shelter hub. Keeping the entire house running during a disaster situation isn't practical, especially if your normal facilities and utilities have been cut off. You want to find a spot in your home that most of your activity will take place in during an emergency. If your power goes out, this is the area you'll be lighting and heating. It's the room you'll be sleeping, preparing food, and eating in.

Many people use their basements or design underground shelters for protection, in areas prone to tornadoes. Most experts say the safest area in the most homes is an interior room above ground. This is important if you're in a region prone to flooding.

You should pick a room that's big enough to fit all of your loved ones and any pets, along with supplies, sleeping bags, blankets, and your non-electrical heating source. Your room should also have quick access to your water and food. If you have a room with a fireplace that might be a good room to choose. It would make heating the room an easier process. This is not the case if you need to seal the house from any contaminated air getting inside. You also need to check if your fireplace requires an electric blower for safety. If it does, you can't use it if the power is out.

If your designated room has a closet, you should clear it out and store all your food, water, fuel, and supplies. If not, choose a room that connects to your designated room. Make sure everyone knows the emergency supplies are only allowed to be used in emergency circumstances.

2. Secure A Water Supply

The next step you must take after securing your shelter is making sure you have the ability to access drinkable water. Without water, you can die within as little as 3 days. Water is easy and inexpensive to stockpile and store securely for an SHTF situation.

Not every disaster will affect the water supply but it's safest to assume that it will. That's why it's best to store plenty of water in advance. You can bottle tap water yourself in advance, collect rainwater and purify it, or buy a supply of bottled water. Buying water is the simplest method and also the most convenient. Collecting rainwater and purifying it is the cheapest but also the most difficult and time-consuming.

Not all containers or bottles are safe for storing your water long-term. Milk containers make bad storage containers. Soda bottles are a better short-term option. They are food grade plastic and UV resistant. I suggest saving 2-liter bottles to fill up. The larger the bottle the better. Once you've stockpiled enough 2-liter bottles, wash each cap and bottle with dish detergent and hot water. Sanitize both your caps and bottles inside and out using a solution of water and bleach. Take 1 teaspoon of household bleach and 1 quart of water. Rinse out the bottles and immediately fill them with your tap water. Place your cap on tight and date the container. Store it in a dark, cool place.

You should try to find space and money to invest in a special water container. They come in many sizes and shapes. These commercial containers come in the form of tanks and drums capable of holding hundreds of gallons of water. You can buy smaller containers that are easily stackable like the WaterBrick or larger tanks that are difficult to set up and almost impossible to move once constructed and filled. You want at least a gallon of water per person for each day you plan on bugging in. Women who are nursing need more water daily. Don't forget water for your pets.

Try to replace your water every six months. While water doesn't go bad it begins to taste stale after being stored for long periods of time. As long as the water has been sanitized and is in a sealed container it can be stored for as long as you want. Still, I prefer the taste of fresh water so I always change out my supply twice a year.

When a disaster occurs, you should fill your bathtubs with water as soon as possible. Do this even if you have enough water stored. This water could be useful if the water remains cut off for a longer than expected, if your well gets contaminated, or your sewage system becomes unavailable.

3. Figure Out How You'll Get Light & Heat

If you own a wood burning fireplace or stove in your shelter room and have not been instructed by emergency officials to seal your house from outside contaminants, you could try to use your stove or fireplace as a source of heat. You must make sure you've gathered firewood for this to be feasible. Check in advance to see if your stove or fireplace can be operated safely without electric powered blowers functioning.

If you don't have a fireplace or stove as a heat source, I suggest investing in portable heaters that don't require electric. These include propane and kerosene. Both are cheap and reliable. They will both keep a small enclosed space warm using only a little fuel. These heaters can be found easily in stores and online. These fuels are sold almost anywhere and can be kept in storage for years on end. Be sure that the heater you purchase is capable of heating the space you're using as your shelter. Test out any heater you purchase to make sure it can adequately do the job. Buy as much fuel as you can store. At a minimum, you should have enough to keep you running for at least 3 days.

Even though you've got a heating source, your work isn't done. That's only a single step in keeping warm while bugging in during an emergency. Once the power goes out, you need to close any doors that access your shelter room and cover the doors with heavy blankets. You need to make sure all of your windows are closed and covered. Try adding heavy blankets over your drapes to improve the insulation. You should shove towels under doors to limit the loss of heat.

Remain physically active in your shelter while bugging in. It will help to keep you warm and it will raise the temperature of the room. Wear clothing in layers. I suggest wearing hats, scarves, gloves, and multiple pairs of socks. Be sure that everyone hunkering down with you has their own set of blankets, comforters, sleeping bag, and quilts. These items should be easy to access in the event of an emergency. The last thing you want is to misplace these items when they are needed the most.

Be sure to have multiple portable light sources in your shelter and the batteries to keep them going. I have a wide variety of portable lanterns, flashlights, candles, headlamps, and neck lamps. These are cheap options that will get the job done. Some of my lights can hold a charge for over a hundred hours at a time. Having plenty of light on hand will make life much simpler during a power outage in an emergency SHTF situation. I always keep at least one of these stored in every room of my house along with a few backups in my storage area.

Candles are cheap and can generate both light and heat. However, they are also a potential fire hazard. I have them as a last option but I don't want to risk using them if I don't have them. This is true for people bugging in with children and pets who don't know better and might accidentally knock them over.

I suggest purchasing a generator powered by gas if it's in your budget. Having one advance is important as they sell out fast leading up to storms and other emergencies. These come in many shapes and sizes. Some are strong enough to power your house and others can help in keeping heaters running and charging your electronics.

4. Stock Your SHTF Food Pantry

Stocking food that's easy to prep and store is a must for possible disaster situations, especially if you reside in a region known for bad snow storms, ice storms, flooding, tornadoes, and other weather situations that can disrupt the electric and halt traffic. Having the necessary supplies to hunker down will go a long way in keeping your family fed and safe even under emergency situations.

The key to a good stockpile is making smart choices. You want to include items with a longer shelf life that don't require special conditions to keep stored, including refrigeration or freezing. These foods should be either easy to prepare or can be eaten right out of the package. That will eliminate items like meat, bread, fresh produce, and dairy which all go bad quickly. Not all food that has a longer shelf life is a candidate for short-term disaster food; dried beans and rice can last a long time but take a lot to prepare.

There is a variety of options for disaster food supplies, including MRE's, and dehydrated food packets. These foods provide all the required nutrition and calories needed to survive and only require water to prepare. These items are portable, compact, and simple to store. These are more expensive than other types of supplies and aren't always available at your local supermarket. Plenty of online retailers carry these items. The most cost-efficient and easiest option is to stock up on vacuum-sealed and canned items. I keep vacuum-stored chicken and tuna in storage, along with canned stews, soups, vegetables, and fruits. These all have a longer shelf life and only require a moderate amount of preparation. Don't forget to have a few can openers stored in your emergency supplies.

I keep canned evaporated milk and fruit juices on hand. It will help to extend your water supplies which is crucial during an emergency. You should also keep powdered milk, instant coffee, tea bags, powdered formula (if you have an infant), and food for your pets. I also store dried items like noodles, oatmeal, soup packets, and standard peanut butter.

When an SHTF situation occurs, eat your normal food first. This includes items like bread, cheese, regular milk, fruit, yogurt, and any meat. Don't dive into your disaster supplies until you need to. If you get lucky, the situation will pass before you run out of food in your refrigerator. If not at least you haven't got a bunch of spoiled food, you need to toss away.

Propane camp stoves are a good choice for heating water in an emergency and cooking food. They are reliable, cheap to buy, come in many sizes, and are fuel efficient. You don't want to use it that often while bugging in since it requires more effort to prepare and clean up after than other types of food required. I suggest storing plenty of plastic knives, forks, spoons, and heavy-duty disposable bowls, cups, and plates. You also want to keep plenty of paper towels, toilet paper, tissues, garbage bags, pain relievers, toothpaste, dry shampoo, deodorant, and hand sanitizer.

5. Establish Your Security Procedures

You need to have a plan for self-defense in case of an emergency. You never know who will come after your supplies during a disaster situation. You want to have a way to defend yourself and family. You should have multiple defensive vantage points mapped out. It's a good idea to plan for a worst-case scenario. At the bare minimum, you should have an escape route planned in case someone makes it into your home.

I installed deadbolts on every door. Consider buying stronger doors that can take a full frontal assault. Your doors should be free of glass and made of steel. You'll want to install a peephole as an additional security measure. I suggest placing locking security grates over each window that can be unlocked from inside, in case you have to escape.

Steps to take include purchasing an extra set of keys to keep with your emergency supplies so you can leave quickly if necessary. Keep the windows and doors locked and covered during an emergency. Make sure your phones are charged and ready to use. Have any weapons in your home prepared and easy to access. Make sure you've trained on how to use them correctly.

During an SHTF situation, the most important thing you can do is remain calm. It's easier said than done but is critical to your safety. If you project a sense of calm, it will spread to the rest of your family. If you panic, your family will pick up on it and panic. Being calm improves your dexterity, memory, response time, resourcefulness, and decision-making skills. All important things when dealing with a crisis.

6. Set Up A Sanitation System

If your sewage system fails, you'll need a way to dispose of your waste. If you have the funds a composting toilet or waterless toilet might be the answer but for most of us, we'll need to find a different way to handle the issue. If you're able to go outside during the emergency that is an option. You'll want to dig a hole at least 6x6 foot at least 200 feet away from any water sources on your property. When finished using it cover it back up with dirt.

If going outside isn't an option, then you'll want to begin by removing as much water as you can from your toilet. Place a heavy garbage bag inside another one and open so you have one double-layer bag. Raise your toilet seat and place the open bag so it fills up most of your toilet. Tape the top of the bag to the underside of your toilet seat. Keep a cat litter bag within reach of your toilet. After using the toilet, cover your waste with cat litter to help mask the smell. Once the bag is more than halfway full, add litter and spray a little disinfectant on it. Take the bag out of the toilet and tie it close. Move the bag to a sealable container (garbage can), that is far from the main shelter area in your house.

Dealing with waste during a no power or no sewage situation is no joke. Failing to properly dispose of waste can lead to terrible living conditions and the risk of serious illnesses. Have a plan in advance to deal with sanitation during an SHTF situation.

7. Staying Positive

It's hard to remain upbeat and positive during a disaster when your loved ones are stuck in a dark, cold, powerless home wondering when and if things will return to normalcy. It's a difficult situation to process emotionally. Being stocked and prepared will go a long way in making things easier and less stressful. However, the longer the situation lasts the larger the toll it will take on you.

It's draining to remain upbeat in a negative situation. You never know if the disaster will last for a day, a week, or a month. The trick is to treat your bug in time like a fun camping vacation. Try sticking to your normal routine as best as possible and keep things light and fun. You need to remain vigilant but enjoy the downtime with your family. You need to expect people to get moody and irritable. Most of us are used to a variety of creature comforts we must make do without during an emergency. Those include television and the Internet.

Get as much rest as you can. Keep as warm as possible and remember to eat enough. I suggest taking a multi-vitamin every day. Remind yourself that everything will be fine and that you're doing everything to keep your loved one's safe and protected.

Chapter Six: Stocking Your SHTF Pantry The Right Way!

Starting Your SHTF Stockpile

Here is a list of preliminary items you'll want to consider when first configuring your stockpile setup.

1. AC Unit - Life without air conditioning is no fun in the heat.

2. Food Grade Buckets - Keep your food safe and dry.

3. Resealable Airtight Containers - Everything needs to be stored and marked clearly with the date of storage, expiration date, and contents. Airtight containers keep your food safe from bacteria and moisture. A nice cheap option.

4. Cleaning Supplies - Dirt and food remnants can lead to pests, bugs, and rodents infesting your pantry. Keep the storage area clean. Animals carry nasty diseases.

5. Shelving - Keep food on shelving and off the floor if possible. I installed heavy-duty shelving. Makes organizing an easier process.

6. Security - Protect your stockpile by keeping it a secret and locking it up. Only the people in your group should have a key and know the location of your stockpiles. The last thing you want is random people knowing about your supplies and stealing them during an SHTF situation.

Once you've figured your stockpile setup and know the items you plan on storing long-term, it's time to purchase the items. Prep as much as your budget and space comfortably allow you to. You should carve out money each month for prepping but don't put yourself into a hole financially trying to get everything at once.

You will never be too prepared. You can always do more. The more preps you have the longer you'll survive with no need to find other sources of food and water. It'll also give you more flexibility when trying to barter for goods and services. The wider variety of things you offer the better your negotiating position. Remember, don't prep items only for barter. You want items your family will use in case no barter situations come into play. The last thing you want is wasted preps. Your prepping plan always needs to be specific to your family and their set of needs.

Here are a few basics you'll want to have in the SHTF stockpile. Other than water and food these items will be useful.

1. Portable Camping Stove / Dutch Oven - Ideal for cooking. Don't forget to stock extra canisters of fuel.

2. Dish Pans - Good for cooking meals, washing dishes, washing clothes, and bathing. Items that fill multiple purposes are perfect for preppers.

3. Multivitamins - Your diet can suffer during a long-term SHTF situation. This will provide the nutrients you might not get otherwise.

4. Garbage Bags - Prep heavy on this item. You want to a variety of different size bags.

5. Lighters / Stick Lighters / Candles - You'll need these for both starting fires and adding additional light.

6. Seeds - Seeds are essential for your long-term health and survival. Start a garden with them and grow food to feed your family indefinitely.

7. Paper Towels / Utensils / Disposable Cups / Paper Cups / Napkins - With little water for cleaning these items will be put to good use. Affordable preps that can be bought in bulk.

8. Can Opener - Having a manual can opener is a must. You should have a few extras stored in your supplies as backups.

9. Hand Mill - Whole grain is great for preppers. It has a ton of nutrients and can be safely stored long-term. However, before using, it needs to be milled. The hand mill does not require you have a power source to use it.

10. Aluminum Foil - Can be used for cooking food over open fires and can help keep food fresh longer.

No stockpile will ever be complete or perfect. However, here is a list of items people serious about prepping should add to their growing SHTF stockpile. This list will differ slightly depending on what your family wants and requires. Most of the items on this list I'd strongly advise to stock up on. They are often the first items to get sold out after an emergency occurs. Better to have it and not use it than not have it and realize you needed it.

1. Water - Necessary for survival. The more you have stocked the better. Always keep a small supply portable and ready to access in case you need to bug out quickly.

2. Prescription Medication - Any medications you or your family are required to take. These are regulated medications and hard to stockpile so you may need to find people to barter or trade with. Try seeking alternatives that don't require a prescription.

3. Pain Medication & Cough Medication - Reducing fevers, pain, soreness, and fevers is important if you want to stay productive and sane. These are the first things to sell out after an emergency so stock up in advance.

4. First Aid Kit - A comprehensive medical kit is vital. In an SHTF situation, you can only rely on yourself and the surrounding people. You need to have supplies on hand for medical emergencies.

5. Batteries - Stock up on all sizes of batteries. Batteries should not be overlooked. They will be needed to make life easier after an emergency.

6. Building Materials - Stockpile assorted materials for future home repairs and new projects. Stockpile screws, lumber, bolts, insulation, and nuts.

7. Alcohol - Used for cooking, disinfecting wounds, and drinking.

8. Backpacks & Bug Out Bags - These are important for making supply runs, going on hunting and scouting trips, and bugging out to new locations.

9. Soap - Keeping clean is important. Getting sick can turn deadly in a disaster. Stockpile both bar soap and liquid soap. You can also learn to make your own soap and stockpile it.

10. Bleach - Important disinfectant to have stocked.

11. Weapons - Keeping your family safe is paramount. Weapons provide protection and the ability to hunt game.

12. Ammo - Guns require ammo. Stock plenty of ammo for the weapons you own. You can also learn to make your own ammo and stockpile it.

13. Blade Sharpener - Blades dull over time and become less effective. Sharpening tools are important to have.

14. Scissors - Often more useful than a knife. Helpful if you plan on making your own clothes at some point.

15. Ax - Ideal for chopping firewood and self-defense. I suggest having a few stockpiled.

16. Salt - Used for adding flavor to food and curing meat.

17. Instant Coffee - Will last indefinitely.

18. Canned Food - One of the main sources of food besides your garden and any game you've caught.

19. Freeze Dried Food - Known as MRE's. Can be stored for a long time until needed.

20. Toothbrushes, Mouthwash, Floss, & Toothpaste - Dental hygiene is important. Tooth pain can be unbearable. I also stock anbesol and amoxicillin for tooth pain and tooth infections.

21. Honey & Sugar - A good source of food that can be stored almost indefinitely. Popular for trade and barter.

22. Canning Supplies - Canning food is important when you're self-reliant. You'll need a stockpile of canning supplies to do that.

23. Cooking Utensils & Tools - Will cut down on cooking time and make the entire process smoother.

24. Firewood - Fuel for fire. Keep plenty chopped and stored safely in a dry place.

25. Feminine Products - A must for women. In addition, good to have for dressing wounds.

26. Charcoal - Helps to save on firewood. A good fuel source for cooking food.

27. Garbage Cans – Trash needs to be contained and kept safe from wildlife before disposal. Also can work as additional storage.

28. Rice, Wheat, Flour, & Beans - Key staple foods. Can help create many dishes.

29. Jerky - Can be stored long-term. Comes in many flavors. Perfect food for stockpiling. You can also learn to make it yourself.

30. Tarps, Rope, Plastic Rolls, Stakes, & Spikes - Will allow you to build safe temporary shelters when needed.

31. Tactical Flashlights, Torches, Lanterns, & Glow Sticks - Portable light sources to help you maneuver around at night.

32. Fuel, Fire Starters, & Oil - Starting a fire is key too long-term survival.

33. Fishing Supplies - Gives you the ability to supplement your food through fishing.

34. Gardening Tools & Supplies - Necessary for managing and growing your garden. Includes items like rakes, shovels, hoes, etc.

35. Milk - Powdered and condensed milk are ideal for stockpiling.

36. Soda, Fruit Drinks, & Gatorade - People need variety. These can be stockpiled for a short time.

37. Books & Guides - Build a library of how-to books and DIY guides. Books should deal with important topics you might face during a disaster. These include home repair books, car repair books, medical journals, gardening books, cookbooks, and survival guides. You won't be able to access information online so if you need to learn something you'll need a book or guide to teach you.

38. Camping Gear - Simplifies traveling. Good for bugging out, fishing trips, scouting trips, and hunting trips.

39. Hunting Apparel, Camouflage, & Body Armor - Being unseen when traveling is important. If someone sees you, they might attack you. Having gear to make you blend into your environment will aid you in hunting and provide you with additional protection. Having strong body armor can help save your life during an attack from both human and animal.

40. Buckets - Keep all shapes and sizes stockpiled. You will find a ton of different uses for these.

41. Carts & Wheelbarrows - Move your heavy loads with ease.

42. Bathroom Supplies - Having items like towels, shampoo, Q tips, and razors will make your life a little better. Proper hygiene will help prevent bacteria growth and sickness.

43. Clothespins, Hangers, & Lines - Used for drying washed clothes. Keeping clothes dry will prevent mold and bacteria growth.

44. Portable Toilets - Without running water you'll want one of these. You can also build an outhouse or purchase a composting toilet.

45. Winter & Outdoor Clothing - Keeping warm and dry during cold season is critical. You want to have clothing for every season and situation.

46. Gloves - Keeping a stockpile of heavy duty gloves is important for the health of your hands. You'll be doing a lot of physical labor and dealing with blisters and injured hands will make life difficult and unpleasant.

47. Work Boots & Shoes - Keep a stockpile of both. Your feet need to be protected.

48. Propane Cylinders - Great fuel source. One of the first items to sell out during an emergency. Perfect item for trade and barter.

49. Duct Tape & Electrical Tape - You will be surprised at all the different uses you find for these items.

50. Rain Gear & Ponchos - Being wet and cold can lead to illness. Stay dry and protected.

51. Solar Panels, Generators, & Wind Turbines - Creating your own source of power will give you a big edge. Will improve your odds of long-term survival. Be careful when using it. Try to keep it hidden or you might become a target.

52. Siphons & Hand Pumps - Ideal for getting gas, oil, and water out of tanks. Great tool for scavenging.

53. Snowmobile - A necessary item if you live in a region prone to lots of snow and harsh winters.

54. Bicycles - Cheap and quick way to get around.

55. Motorcycles - Ideal for short to medium trips. Requires less gas than a car and easy to navigate.

56. Chainsaw - Great for cutting down bigger trees and cutting wood for projects.

57. Fire Extinguishers - Good f you need to put out a fire quickly. Without one you might lose your home and all your preps from a single incident.

58. Tools - Having a good supply of screwdrivers, hammers, vices, wrenches, etc. will make projects easier to accomplish.

59. Mosquito Coils & Repellent - Protection from getting eaten alive by mosquitoes and bugs.

60. Personal Items - Having backups for important personal items is crucial. For example, if you need glasses have a few backup pairs stored. If you wear dentures have another set created and a stockpile of denture adhesive.

61. Protein Drinks & Protein Bars - Easy sources of needed daily nutrients.

62. Dried Fruits, Fruit Strips, & Raisins - Good items for long-term storage.

63. Hard Cheeses (Encased In Wax) - Wax prevents your cheese from growing bacteria and mold. Cheese can be stored for years in wax.

64. Jellies & Jams - Good food items to stockpile. Popular item for trade and barter.

65. Dried Pasta - Good food item to stockpile. Easy to prepare and a good source of carbohydrates.

66. Inflatable Mattresses & Cots - Spare bedding is important.

67. Humidifier - Reduce moisture in your stockpile pantry room. Bacteria grows when moisture accumulates in small areas.

68. Window Insulation Kits - You want all the heat to remain in your house not leak outside of it.

69. Mousetraps, Ant Traps, & Rat Poison - Stop infestation before it spirals out of control.

70. Coleman Mantles - Ideal for long-term lighting.

71. Sewing Fabric & Supplies - Useful for making and mending clothes.

72. Livestock - Start small in advance and learn to raise and breed them before a disaster strikes. Important for long-term survival after an SHTF situation.

73. Toilet Paper - One luxury I don't want to live without.

74. Animal Feed & Pet Food - If you raise livestock or have a pet you can't forget to stock the items they'll need.

75. Chewing Gum, Hard Candy, Survival Tabs, & Lip Balm - All helpful survival items to keep handy.

76. Journals, Calendars, Scrapbooks, & Diaries - Keep track of time, write thoughts, remember important occasions, and keep a log of your supplies and preps.

77. Writing Materials (Pencils / Pens) - Can be used for tracking your supplies, scheduling tasks and projects, and writing your thoughts.

78. Games - Entertainment is important. Board games, books, cards, magazines, and dice can all add a little fun to your life.

Item to Stockpile With a Higher Barter Value

Many of these items will overlap with the above list. I keep a certain amount of the items on this list in a separate stockpile, with the intent of bartering. Avoid bartering with items you and your loved ones currently need. You never know if you'll be able to find an item again.

1. Gold & Silver - Currency if an SHTF situation occurs. I keep a small stockpile.

2. Alcohol - People want their booze and will barter to get it.

3. Power - Solar power kits become valuable items to own once the grid goes dark.

4. Cigarettes - People want their nicotine and will barter to get it.

5. Water - People who need water will pay a big price for yours.

6. Ice - If you have the ability to create and store ice you'll have a valuable commodity for barter.

7. Weapons - People understand the importance of defense. Weapons will fetch a premium.

8. Ammo - People can always use extra bullets for their weapons.

9. Fuel - Fuel is a critical resource for people looking to operate generators and vehicles.

10. Batteries - People want to power smaller handheld items. Batteries make that possible.

11. Medicine - Medicine can mean the difference between life and death. It will garner a high premium.

12. Canning Lids - A key part of preserving your food long-term.

13. Toilet Paper - A luxury I'm not willing to part with which can make it valuable to others that feel the same way.

14. Seeds - Growing food is important for long-term survival. This will require seeds. This makes them ideal for bartering.

15. Camping Supplies - People need tents, sleeping bags, and camping gear if they plan on taking overnight hunting or fishing trips.

16. Candles - Candles illuminate the night. No one wants to live in total darkness for 12 hours a day.

17. Meat - If you raise your own livestock and are blessed with extra meat you'll find many people willing to barter.

18. Vegetables - You can trade for goods and items you need with your surplus crops.

19. Milk & Cheese - Fresh cheese and milk will always fetch a high premium.

20. Detergent - Clean clothes is a little thing that many people will pay extra for.

21. Water Filters - Clean water is a necessity. Water filters will make cleaning your water much easier.

22. Battery Operated Radio - Ideal for people who want updates after an SHTF situation occurs.

23. Canned Food - Canned foods are popular items to add to stockpiles. Easy to store and will last long-term.

24. Sugar, Salt, & Honey - Staple foods many people aren't willing to live without.

25. Tools - Extra hammers, saws, and wrenches to barter with will fetch you a solid price.

26. Marijuana - People suffering from medical conditions will pay anything to relieve their pain. A good bartering item in an emergency.

27. Clothing & Sewing Supplies - The ability to make your own clothes can allow you to barter clothes for items you need.

28. Building Supplies - Home repairs and new projects will always be necessary. If you have extra supplies like nails, screws, and lumber you'll be in a nice spot.

29. Skills & Knowledge - Trade your skills and knowledge for items you need.

30. Entertainment - Board games, books, and toys will be a popular item to barter among parents with smaller kids.

Chapter Seven: Key Survival Skills & Projects

Key Survival Skills

Once you've made your plans and started stockpiling, you need to master the skills needed to survive an SHTF situation long-term. Here are the key survival skills you'll want to consider learning to increase your odds of survival. Decide the importance of these skills and work on them from most to least important.

1. Lock Picking - If you live in an urban area this skill could be valuable. Being able to pick locks will allow you to access places most people won't be able to get into. This includes areas to shelter in and areas to scavenge for food.

2. Knot Tying - This skill will allow you to do things like making traps for hunting game, operate sailboats, secure outdoor shelters, and create a fishing rig.

3. Hunting - The ability to hunt game will increase your odds of survival. Learn what animals live in your region and where they can be located. Learn to track animals, set traps, and fish. You should learn what plants are edible and inedible.

4. First Aid - Take first aid and CPR classes. At a bare minimum learn to bandage and treat wounds. You should always keep medical manuals and a first aid kit in your stockpile. Learn how to use the items you've stockpiled.

5. Water Purifying - You need to learn this skill. Water sources can become contaminated for a variety of reasons. If you can't purify your water, you may run into trouble.

6. Clothing Repair - The ability to repair and make clothing is a useful skill to have. You'll need clothes to brave the elements. Learning to sew will go a long way.

7. Starting Fires - You should be able to start a fire using multiple methods. You should be able to start a fire with none of your normal fire starting tools. You also need to learn how to keep your fire going once it's started.

8. Weapons Training - If you own a weapon for defense you need to know how to use it and store it. I suggest taking classes on weapon safety and going to the firing range to practice.

9. Self Defense Training - Learning hand to hand combat could save you in an SHTF situation. If someone gets the jump on you and your family, you need to know how to defend yourself and disarm your attacker.

10. Building A Shelter - Learn to take the items available to you and turn them into a safe shelter. You'll need this skill if you ever need to bug out.

11. Gardening & Composting - Learning to garden and compost is vital to your long-term survival. Growing food will allow you to thrive off-grid. It will make up most of your diet once your stockpile runs low.

12. Navigation - Learning to read maps and navigate by the sun and stars can help you survive if you ever get lost when bugging out, hunting, or fishing.

13. Cooking - You won't be able to order out or hit the grocery store during an SHTF situation. Learn how to cook food from scratch. Learn to cure meat, make your own bread, cheese, and alcohol. You should learn to dehydrate and preserve your food. You should also learn how to can your supplies. Take a few culinary classes to sharpen your general cooking skills.

14. Backyard Beekeeping - Learning to tend bees will provide you with a consistent supply of honey. Honey is a valuable item for barter. It can be used for food and making items like candles.

15. Building - Learning carpentry is a useful skill to have after an SHTF situation. When you're cut off from the world, you'll be responsible for building what you need and fixing what breaks. I would learn as many building skills as you can.

16. Mechanical Repair - Learning how to work on your equipment is important. Someone needs to maintain your vehicles and any equipment you used to run your household. You should understand the basics of car repair along with how to change your tires, oil, and brake pads. If you can't fix your vehicle and you get stranded, it could cost you your life.

17. Raising Livestock - You should consider learning how to care and raise livestock. They can provide a constant source of meat, eggs, milk, cheese, and wool depending on the animals you raise. You'll want to learn how to breed these animals and butcher them. You'll also want to learn first aid for animals. If your livestock gets sick, you need to know how to care for them and prevent further illnesses. A single outbreak could kill all your livestock.

Helpful Project Ideas SHTF Preppers Should Do

Here are a few ideas for projects that will help you survive after an SHTF situation. You might not need all of these depending on the length and type of emergency you're dealing with. It will also depend on your living situation. You might be an urban prepper or have a lot of land. Depending on the region you live in you must worry about different terrain, weather patterns, and the number of people living around you.

1. Build your water storage.

2. Build storage for your firewood. Firewood will take time to cure and dry. Keep a large enough supply to get you through the winter months.

3. Build a chicken coop. Breeding and raising chickens is a constant source of food.

4. Build a rocket stove. A great tool for cooking.

5. Build yourself a triple compost bin. Will give you nutrient-rich soil for your garden.

6. Build a garden. Plan out what crops you want to grow. This will be a primary source of food for your family.

7. Build a honey cow to keep bees for wax and honey production.

8. Build an outhouse. Ideal if you don't have access to running water.

9. Build a solar food dryer. Ideal for dehydrating food.

10. Build a water filter. You need to clean your water before purifying it.

11. Build furniture. Can be used in your home and as an item for barter.

12. Build tools and a wooden cart. This will make tasks and chores easier to finish.

Chapter Eight: Tips & Tricks for Being Prepared When SHTF

Tips & Tricks for Being Prepared When SHTF

1. Have multiple bug out locations you can fall back to in an emergency. Each location should have its own stockpile.

2. Keep your empty bottles for additional water storage. Small containers are ideal for travel.

3. Plan all your escape routes in advance. Practice each one and have a bug out bag located nearby for easy access.

4. Practice firing and cleaning your weapons. Go to the firing range and run safety drills.

5. Install security measures on your property. Secure your windows and doors. Consider adding strike plates to any exterior doors.

6. Practice different first aid scenarios. Knowing how to handle different medical emergencies will come in handy during an SHTF situation.

7. Keep your vehicles accessible. Leave a bug out bag in your trunk.

8. Run emergency drills every month. The calmer you are in the face of danger the higher your odds of survival. Drilling will point out the areas you need to improve and what things you're doing well. Have your drills at different times of the day. You want to practice running all your drills during both daytime and nighttime hours.

9. Never stop prepping. There are always things to be done. Don't forget to set up your system for rotating preps in and out before old preps reach their expiration date.

10. Tell no one your prepping plans. Only your family and people in your group should know your preps and plans for an SHTF situation. You can't risk people trying to steal your stuff during a disaster.

11. If you ever get injured, a little toilet paper and duct tape can be fashioned into a splint to aid you in setting a broken bone.

12. Crayons can create an emergency candle.

13. Your generator needs to be in a well guarded and safe area. These will be targeted by thieves after a disaster. Only use your generator when it is necessary and conceal it as best as possible.

14. You can add apple cider to your livestock water or food to aid in boosting their immunity.

15. Baby oil on your skin can help negate the effects of frostbite.

16. Build your library. The more DIY guides, medical books, gardening books, and cookbooks you own the better. These books can help to fill in the information gap of skills you haven't already gained or mastered.

17. Build a stockpile of firewood. You need to find a dry space to store it long-term. Having firewood stocked will ease some stress after an emergency. You need a way to heat your shelter and cook your food. Firewood is the answer to both issues.

18. Get creative and turn your 5-gallon buckets into a chicken feeder.

19. Poke holes into the lids of your 1-gallon jugs and turn them into a watering can.

20. Invest in precious metals and other items that can be used for barter. I convert a little each month to precious metals. I carved out space in my budget to do this. If the world collapses your bank accounts will disappear and your paper money will become worthless. People will still recognize the value of gold, silver, diamonds, supplies, and food. Those will become the new currencies.

21. Duct tape can help you open your jars with minimal effort.

22. Find other preppers and build a tight-knit community. Surviving is easier when you have people who think like you and can be of service.

23. You can turn your empty 2-liter soda bottles into storage containers for foods like beans and rice.

24. You should start a collection of different seeds you want to plant in your future garden. A garden can take time to dial in so be sure to continue prepping your SHTF storage pantry.

25. Eggs can be frozen to stop them from going bad.

26. Build something to store your ice. Ice will allow you to store vegetables and meat for longer periods of time. It will go a long way in extending the life of your SHTF pantry.

27. Routinely maintenance your weapons, vehicles, and home. Don't allow things to fall into disrepair. You never know when an emergency will occur.

28. You can take parts from an old bike and turn them into a crossbow for hunting.

29. Begin a physical fitness routine. Surviving an SHTF situation will require a lot of physical effort. Whether it's work maintaining your homestead or traveling to a new bug out location carrying your supplies. Doing everything yourself is a difficult life. You need to be in the best shape possible to withstand it.

30. Keep multiple caches for your assorted preps. If you keep everything in a single location, you could face trouble if that spots becomes compromised.

31. Baking powder and baking soda can help remove stains, eliminate bad odors, and clean sinks and counters.

32. To warm up a small area of ground for planting crops use a little black plastic sheeting.

33. Your eyeglasses can start a fire. The glasses can magnify the sun and ignite the tinder underneath.

34. Purchase a few bikes and smaller-sized trailers to attach to them. This can make it a breeze to transport items back and forth from any nearby neighbors and to different parts of your property.

35. Save up any coffee grounds. They are great for using as plant food, in compost, and as a deodorizer for your refrigerator and hands.

36. You can turn a tarp and a few lightweight branches into a working raft.

37. Never use untreated water when cleaning your wounds. Don't run your hands under untreated water if they have any cuts or wounds on them. If you do, it will open you to a variety of bacterial infections.

38. When traveling, always keep a little aluminum foil in your pack. It's perfect for laying on damp ground to create a dry platform to start a fire over.

39. You can use bleach to purify water. The ratio is 2 drops of unscented bleach for 1 liter of water.

40. Lay your tent pegs across a couple of logs and quickly turn it into a temporary grill.

41. A jar of Crisco can create a temporary candle.

42. Don't keep water in your old milk containers. Milk residue is tough to clean out and may lead to unhealthy bacteria forming in your water.

43. Try to test everything personally every other month. This goes for any tools, weapons, camping gear, fishing gear, cooking gear, and vehicles. If something isn't functioning you need to know in advance so you can either fix or replace it before you need it for something.

44. If you have a Zippo lighter that runs out of fuel it can still start a fire. Take the cotton located inside the lighter and use its flint to start a spark that will ignite your cotton.

45. You should place masking tape on the lens of your flashlight to reduce the overall profile. This will give you enough light to complete your task but keep your presence less detectable to other people.

46. Learn to navigate by the stars at night. Knowing a few constellations can help you quickly figure out the direction you need to head towards.

47. If you own pets or livestock don't forget to include them in your prepping plans. They will require their own stockpile of supplies.

48. Toothpaste is wonderful for treating bug bites and insect stings.

49. You can turn a garbage bag into a temporary rain jacket by cutting holes out for your head and arms.

50. If you can't afford to purchase a stab-resistant body armor vest you can create a homemade one using carbon steel saws. Combine your saws using duct tape to form a thick stab proof plate you can insert into a vest for some additional protection.

51. Understand any state and local laws. Different places have different ordinances and laws regarding what you can prep and how much you can store. For instance, lots of areas have restrictions on the amount of firewood you can keep stored on your property. You don't want to get fined or face legal problems because you didn't know what was and wasn't allowed.

52. If dealing with wet and soggy conditions, you can find tinder by shaving off strips from twigs and logs.

53. Keep a few water purifying tablets in your bag when traveling. If you can't start a fire and boil your water you can use these instead.

54. If you place a few big rocks around your fire it will help to absorb some of heat. Once the fire dies down your rocks will still give off heat and can keep you feeling warm.

55. Keep a few glow sticks in your bag when traveling. You can tie them to a piece of paracord and create a big light in case you become lost and need rescuing from the rest of your party.

56. The entrails of animals make good bait for your traps, snares, and fishing bait.

57. A disposable poncho can work as both a rain coat and temporary shelter. You can also create a solar still from them to gather and purify your water.

58. When packing your bug out bag place the lighter stuff on bottom and the heavier stuff at the top. It will help give you a better center of gravity.

59. When processing any game you've caught do it away from your home. It will help you avoid attracting unwanted animals from coming to your door.

60. If you need a sharp edge and don't have your knife, you can smash a couple of rocks together.

61. You don't need to waste time chopping each log with your axe. You can snap them using force or kick them in half. Unless it's for a project that requires precision and exact measurements.

62. I always keep a pack of cigarettes in my bag. It can be used as a small gift if you meet new people or given to calm down someone in your party who smokes.

63. When sleeping in a temporary shelter don't lay directly on the ground. This will remove the heat from your body quicker than if you create a small-sized platform of logs or sticks you can rest your sleeping bag on.

64. You can increase the heat within your temporary shelter by duct taping a foil blanket to the inside of your shelter.

65. Always waterproof your gear in advance. You should waterproof as much of your equipment as possible.

66. Set up your camp in an area that is elevated and away from the nearest water source. Water will draw more insects and animals.

67. If you need to close a wound in an emergency try using super glue.

68. If you form a blister, thread a needle through the blister. Leave the thread in to soak up moisture and keep it open. Take duct tape and put over the blister. This will eliminate any friction and stop further blisters from occurring.

69. Try to avoid tobacco when bugging out or traveling. Tobacco can decrease stamina by limiting the amount of oxygen and blood flowing to your brain.

70. Keep currency in your bug out bag. You should always have currency with you when traveling in case you need to barter and pay for something.

71. If you're physically active wear fewer clothes. If you're continually moving and drop all the layers you'll still feel comfortable. Sweating in cold weather can lead to wet clothes and the chance of hypothermia.

72. Drink milk from green coconuts only. Older coconuts and ripe coconuts contain more of an oil that acts as a laxative. You don't want to risk dehydration due to diarrhea.

73. Socks will work as a filter to remove dirt and debris from water.

74. Get rid of the unnecessary items in your home. You want space for supplies and preps. Evaluate what you need and cut down on the items that don't add value to your life.

75. Come up with a system of hand signals to communicate with your family in silence. If an emergency occurs, this can come in handy.

76. Stock up on lumber. You want wood stored away for projects you might want to construct in the future. Get all different sizes.

77. Dip your cotton balls into petroleum jelly and place in small-sized plastic bags. Work as an easy fire starter.

78. Don't drink an excess amount of water when you have an empty stomach. It can disrupt your electrolytes and lead to shock.

79. If an animal drinks from a water source it doesn't mean it's safe for human consumption. Animals can eat and drink things poisonous to us.

80. Always keep an everyday kit in your possession. This should include items like a lighter, multi-tool, knife, and cash.

81. Know the amount of ammunition you have. You need to know if you're running low so you can procure more before you run out.

82. Take your bathes using rainwater. Don't use your storage water for bathing, washing clothes, or washing dishes.

83. Smoke will naturally repel insects. Wave your gear and clothes in smoke to help prevent insect bites.

84. After assembling you bug out bag practice wearing it around your house to get used to the weight. It will give you a good idea if you've packed too much or if you can handle carrying the weight for long periods of time.

85. When bugging out trust your instincts. If something doesn't feel right keep moving. Don't stay somewhere if your instinct is telling you to go.

86. Have a few sets of Walkie Talkies so you're able to communicate with your group over short distances.

87. Plan out a system for disposing of your waste. You need to have a good plan in place for waste disposal or things will get messy quick.

88. Dispose of garbage right away. You can burn it or bring it to a different location. Letting your garbage pile up will attract rodents and pests.

89. Enjoy the time you get to spend with your family and friends. Off-grid living is hard. Embrace happiness whenever possible.

Chapter Nine: Building an SHTF Weapons Cache & Defending Your Family

Guide to Gun Safety

When planning for an SHTF emergency you'll want to consider purchasing a gun to protect your family and defend your home. If you purchase a gun, you need to learn the proper way to operate it, clean it, and store it.

Four rules for operating and owning your gun:

1. Treat your gun like it's loaded at all times. Even if the gun is empty.

2. Don't point your gun muzzle at a target unless you plan on shooting it.

3. Don't put your finger on the gun trigger until you will shoot.

4. Know your target and what lies beyond the target in the event you miss your shot.

Let's take a further look at each of the rules:

1. Treat your gun like it's loaded at all times. Even if the gun is empty.

You need to treat your weapon like it's always loaded. Check your weapon before handling it. Discipline is key when handling a gun. If you lack discipline accidents can happen. Don't risk the safety of yourself or those around you. You bear responsibility for any injuries that occur from accidentally discharging your weapon. Practice being safe until it becomes a part of you. A common mistake I hear about is people forgetting to check the chamber. You need to check the chamber to see if there's a round still in there. This is one of the leading causes of accidental gun deaths.

2. Don't point your gun muzzle at a target unless you plan on shooting it.

Remaining focused is important. Many gun owners will accidentally discharge their weapon at some point. This is why it's important not to point the muzzle of your gun at a target unless you plan on shooting it. The muzzle is the part of the gun where the bullet exits when fired. The other end of the gun where the bullet goes in is called the breech. Never wave your weapon around. Bad habits are easy to pick up. Try to keep the muzzle of your gun safely pointed away from people.

3. Don't put your finger on the gun trigger until you will shoot.

Don't keep your finger resting on the gun trigger. The only time your finger should be on the trigger is when you're about to shoot your weapon. Resting one's finger on the gun trigger is a big cause of accidental discharges. If you're walking around with your finger resting on the trigger and you trip or stumble, you could end up shooting someone accidentally. I've heard a few of these stories firsthand. Keep your finger resting on the gun frame above the trigger guard. This will help prevent you from discharging by accident.

4. Know your target and what lies beyond the target in the event you miss your shot.

Bullets will travel a long distance once fired. If you don't hit your target you don't want to hit someone else behind them. Always check what lies beyond your target before pulling the trigger.

Improving Your Gun Skills

Having a weapon is only helpful if you know how to operate it. Self-defense is much more chaotic and stressful than target shooting. When your life is on the line, you must act fast. Being trained to handle this kind of situation is of the utmost importance. Here are ways you can help sharpen your weapon skills.

1. Pick The Perfect Gun - You want a weapon that works for you. Try to shoot a few different caliber guns and decide which is most comfortable. Don't buy a gun before testing that gun type at a shooting range. I made that mistake and ended up having to return the gun I purchased to buy one that was a better fit.

2. Practice Makes Perfect - Learn how to clean, store, and fire your weapon. The gun should feel like an extension of yourself. When dealing with an SHTF situation, you need to react without thinking. Take classes with certified instructors and go to the range monthly to practice.

3. Keep Focus on Your Target - Don't look down when reloading or shooting. Keep focused on the target at all times. Practice this until it becomes second nature. In an emergency, you always need to be focused on the target. Distraction could have devastating consequences.

4. Shoot With Either Hand - You should learn to fire your weapon with both hands. You can't predict what might happen in an emergency. You might only have the option of firing with one hand. If that hand is the non-dominant hand you want to have as much experience shooting with it as possible.

5. Shoot Fast & Be Accurate - Hitting the intended target fast could keep you alive. You need to have a combination of speed and accuracy when firing your gun.

6. Practice Firing On Targets That Move - You need to mimic real-life scenarios when practicing your shooting. Your target won't remain stationary in real-life. You want to learn how to hit targets coming from all angles and positions. You should also practice shooting from your stomach and from your knees.

7. Dummy Ammo Only - Practice loading and unloading your gun with different magazines and dummy ammo. You don't want to fumble around when loading your gun in an emergency. You'd be surprised how many people forget to practice the little things. Details matter.

8. Practice Using Your Holster - You want to get good at drawing your weapon from your holster. You need to draw both cleanly and quickly. If you can't remove your gun from its holster in time, you might not have a chance to shoot your target before getting shot yourself.

9. Dry Run Fire Drills - Practice at home with an unloaded weapon. Go through all the safety checks to make sure the gun isn't loaded before practicing. Visualize targets and scenarios while drawing your weapon and pretending to fire. Nothing beats real target practice, but this is a good training aid to sharpen your skills further.

10. Learn to Use a Gun Safe - If you have a break-in or an emergency occurs, you must access your weapon fast. Not knowing how to operate your gun safe could end up putting your safety in jeopardy. Run drills to practice removing your weapon from the gun safe. Time yourself and work on beating previous records.

Preparing Your Arsenal

When deciding on your arsenal you need more than just weapons. Don't forget you also need to store ammo, cleaning supplies to care for the weapons, safes and cases to store the weapons, and spare parts to fix weapons that wear down or become damaged. I suggest including several different weapons in your arsenal. I love my pistol and shotgun but those are far from the only weapons I keep stored.

Here is what my arsenal comprises and why I chose these weapons.

1. Pistol - The primary weapon I carry. Good for both self-defense and hunting small game.

2. Shotgun - Cheap ammunition and simple to operate. Good for both self-defense and hunting.

3. Semi-Automatic Rifle - Ideal for hunting and shooting at long range.

4. Knives - I carry a small pocketknife. I also own an assortment of larger hunting knives.

5. Hunting Bow & Arrows - I keep a hunting bow for tracking bigger game. This is a skill I'm still a novice at.

6. Sprays - I store both bear spray and pepper spray.

7. Ammunition - I keep approximately 2000 rounds of ammo stored for each weapon. I'm still adding to my ammunition stockpile because it's good for both defense and bartering.

8. Cleaning supplies - I keep all the supplies needed to clean each weapon along with instructional repair books.

9. Spare Parts - I keep spare parts to build at least two more of each gun I own.

10. Gun Safes, Cases, & Cabinets - Large weapons stay locked inside my gun cabinet. I keep my two pistols in separate gun safes in different parts of my house. I own a variety of gun cases for when I need to travel with my guns. Your guns should always be locked away when not in use.

11. Holsters - I keep spare gun holsters for each of my weapons. Never know when you might need a replacement.

12. Bean Bag Gun - This is an option for people who don't want to own a gun but still value being protected. A bean bag gun will allow you to take down an intruder long enough to subdue them or flee from them in an emergency. These weapons can be gas powered and spring loaded. They will do serious non-lethal damage when fired.

13. Taser - Another good weapon for disabling attackers. Tasers are effective up to around 30 feet. It should stop your attacker for a minimum of 5 seconds. It should allow you time to subdue your attacker or flee the scene.

14. Stun Gun - This weapon will hit them with enough current to stop an attacker dead in their tracks. The longer you hit them with the stun gun the more damage it will cause. Another good choice for people either not allowed to own guns or who choose not to own them.

15. Baseball Bat - Simple yet effective. A good aluminum or wooden bat can do a lot of damage. Anyone can use this weapon without training which makes it ideal for people who don't practice with weapons. An aluminum bat is preferred as it is more durable and can cause more damage than a wooden one.

16. Mace & Pepper Spray - Great for close contact. Spray into your attacker's eyes and blind them temporarily. Very painful and a good item to carry whenever you leave your home.

Defending The Home

Keeping your family safe at home during an SHTF emergency is a big priority when bugging in. You should always have a plan in place ready to go should the time come you need to defend your home.

Depending on where you live, you might be under a lot of duress from nearby individuals looking to take your preps and supplies. There are ways you can help make it safer for your family at home. I will go over a few of the options. Before using any of what I suggest, make sure it's legal to do so where you live. Certain areas have ordinances and laws on what is allowed and not allowed on your property.

1. Deter intruders from even thinking of trespassing. You can install signs on your property warning that "trespassers will get shot", "nothing here worth dying for", or "beware of dogs". You'd be surprised at the effect a sign can have on the human psyche. It tells attackers you won't be an easy target. I know if I see a sign about a dog I'm not stepping foot on that property if I can help it.

2. Set up an alarm system that lets attackers and you both know their trespassing. You can install fencing, motion detectors, audible alarms, trip wires, cameras, and barbed wire to scare off trespassers.

3. You can set up traps around your home. You can dig out pits along your property and place wooden stakes underneath. Just cover the hole with leaves, twigs, and light branches. You can also set up bear traps to stop an attacker. Place nail beds in random spots and cover with twigs. Always be sure everyone who has access to your property knows about the traps and their locations. You wouldn't want an accident to occur.

4. Fortify your home. Add stronger security steel doors to all your entrances. These will come with door braces and deadbolts for additional security. Add removable bars to your windows. Treat your windows with security film so they become hard to break. Swap out your windows with non-breakable Plexiglas. You can also place chicken wire or barbed wire around your outer windows to make them harder to access.

5. Buy guard dogs for your property. A well-trained guard dog can be a big asset in protecting your home. Dogs are light sleepers and will be the first to realize an intruder has made their way on to your property.

6. Have weapons easy to access in your home in case of an emergency. If someone gets through all of your defenses you want to be prepared to fight them off with force.

7. Build in secret safe rooms to hide people and supplies from would-be attackers. Modified closets work well.

8. Have a supply of sandbags and sand in your storage. These can be placed behind your doors during an attack to fortify them further and prevent attackers from getting inside. These are also good at absorbing gunfire. Sandbags are cheap and easy to move around.

9. Build a bunker under your home with escape routes off your property. This is a little extreme but I know people who have these. They keep all their preps in their bunker and will wait out an attack underneath the home pretending the house was abandoned.

Conclusion

I appreciate you checking out my book. I hope that you've realized the importance of SHTF prepping and are ready to take steps toward becoming better prepared and better protected.

The ability to survive on only your skills and resolve during an emergency is something you can take pride in even if an SHTF situation never occurs. The lessons and different skills discussed in this guide aren't only ideal for protection, they're also good for teaching you about nature and lowering your bills through self-sustainability.

While there's no way to predict what will happen, I know that by prepping and training for the worst I'll be putting myself in the best spot possible. That's all one can hope for when disaster strikes.

Made in the USA
Middletown, DE
05 July 2025

10155026R00060